Dollarstore Quiet Bins

Nine dollarstore items, 30 brilliant Quiet Bins

Sarah Noftle, BA, B. Ed.

Dollarstore Quiet Bins

Nine dollarstore items, 30 brilliant quiet bins.

Disclaimer: Some of these Quiet Bins contain small parts. Supervise any young children while using these bins.

Photography by Sarah Noftle.

Contents

Why Quiet Bins?

If you have read my first book, *A Year of Educational Quiet Bins: The secret to peaceful days at home with kids,* you already know the answer to this question.

When I was first home with my busy, busy boys I was struggling. Really struggling.

We were missing an important rhythm to our day, which I discuss in detail in that first book. I won't go through all of those details again—the why, what, and how of establishing a rhythm—but I will say that Quiet Bins are still essential to our peaceful days.

When my little boys have been busy playing outside, start to get a little too rambunctious, or are struggling with that awful dinnertime witching hour, Quiet Bins still save our day.

Quiet Bins help little ones transition out of a busy time, which can be a challenge for them to do on their own. It provides them with a focus for their energy, allowing them to slow down, calm down, and rest their bodies.

Quiet Bins also help those little ones who are out of naps but still need a time of quiet in the afternoon. They help these little ones settle, relax, and rest.

Quiet Bins, equally importantly, give parents and care-givers this same time for rest and calm, as each bin can be done independently by children.

Why these 9 dollarstore Items?

If you are reading this book, you are busy. This book is intended for parents, caregivers, and teachers of little ones between the ages of 2-6 years old.

Anyone who is surrounded by little ones of that age is busy! I know first hand that you do not have the time to be driving all over town to get supplies for Quiet Bins.

As well, having little ones can get expensive. Keeping the cost of supplies for these Quiet Bins to a minimum was important to me.

So, I have thought of the 9 most used supplies in my home. These supplies can be purchased very inexpensively and from virtually any Dollarstore.

I really believe you will be able to make all 30 of these Quiet Bins for $10 worth of supplies at the Dollarstore. Of course you might need to add a few more here and there, and a few of the bins require you to cut cupcake liners and such, but all in all I am thrilled with the result.

Oodles of ideas, next to no preparation, and a very low budget.

As well, the supplies themselves are powerful for little ones to use.

Clothespins and rubber bands are fabulous for strengthening little hands for future writing.

Holding and playing with popsicle sticks and straws can in fact work on pencil grips

Pompoms and buttons are great for improving fine motor skills

Cupcake liners and paper plates help little ones with sorting and cutting skills.

And pipecleaners are the best of the best as far as supplies for Quiet Bins go. They strengthen little hands, work on lots of different hand muscles, develop fine motor skills, hand-eye coordination, and bend in lots of ways to promote creativity and problem solving.

Lots of opportunities for learning and growing with just a little bit of time and resources—just what a parent with little ones needs.

How to get the most out of Quiet Bins

I have worked with, lived with, and taught children for over 13 years now. I am a certified teacher and have become a Reading Specialist as well as holding additional qualifications in Special Education. And yet, I cannot teach young children better than they can teach themselves.

I know that probably sounds bizarre, but it is completely true. The best thing I can do as a teacher and a parent is to set up an awesome learning environment, give my little ones great invitations to play, and provide them with meaningful experiences.

And so with that knowledge, I suggest you let these bright little ones explore these Quiet Bins in any way they choose.

If they opt to create race cars out of the flower making Quiet Bin—brilliant. If they decide to build the tallest tower that has ever been built out of the bracelet making supplies—fabulous.

I would even suggest you present the Quiet Bins to little ones completely open-ended. Just give them the box and say, "Here you go!" and then you go too— have a coffee, tea, or glass of wine (depending on the day you've had).

Trust your little ones will be learning and growing ever more independent and creative with each Quiet Bin.

Of course you can later sit beside them and offer suggestions for how to use the Quiet Bin, helping to stretch their limits and support their growth. There is certainly a time and place for this as well. I'm sure you will feel when it's the right time to offer some support or structure.

I really believe that little ones need loads of time to explore and play, and these Quiet Bins are a great means to that end.

Introducing Letters

Some of these Quiet Bins include introducing little ones to the alphabet, matching uppercase and lowercase letters, and even building words.

If you have a little one who is just about to learn his or her letters, or who is quite young, I would strongly suggest beginning with his or her name. These letters are very important and hold meaning to your child, making them a fabulous place to start.

Begin with your child's name as he would see it written—a capital for the first letter and lowercase for the others. After he is really comfortable with these letters, add in the uppercase letters to match and allow lots of time to play with these. This will let your little one understand that there are two types of letters—uppercase and lowercase—both making the same sounds, just used in different ways.

After your child really, really knows those name letters, introduce the other letters in chunks. I use an order similar to that of Jolly Phonics. You can find out exactly why I do that over on my blog (right here: http://www.howweelearn.com/teaching-letter-recognition-what-order-to-introduce-letters/). Here is the order I suggest:

The Order for Teaching Letter Recognition

www.HowWeeLearn.com

1. s, a, t, i, p, n
2. c, k, e, h, r
3. m, d, g, o
4. l, f, b, q, u
5. j, z, w
6. v, y, x

"Behind every young child who believes in himself, is a parent who believed first."

-Matthew Jacobson

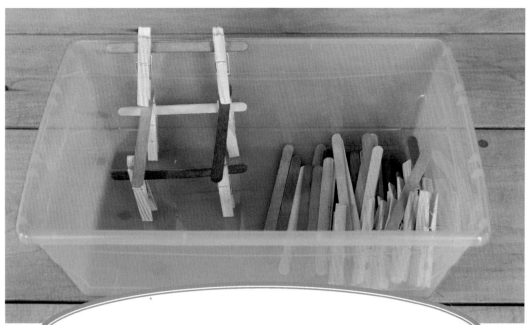

Building with Clothespins and Popsicle Sticks

Materials:

- Popsicle Sticks

- Clothespins

Target skills:

- Fine motor skills

- Creative thinking and problem solving skills

- STEM skills

Building is a fabulous activity for young children. They can create so many different structures, while learning so many different skills.

Building with blocks is great, but this Quiet Bin takes it up a notch. Little ones can build long roads or high towers with these two simple supplies.

Offering the bin with no instructions allows little ones to create and build on their own accord.

After a little while, you may wish to show how the pieces can fit together as a tower if your little one hasn't figured it out.

Popsicle Stick Puppets

Materials:

- Popsicle sticks with faces

- Pipecleaners cut in half

Target skills:

- Strengthening hands for writing

- Imaginative play

Puppets were the forgotten about toy around here. That was until this Quiet Bin made its appearance.

My little ones love wrapping the pipecleaners to make arms and legs for people, or paws and ears for pets.

The best part of this Quiet Bin is all of the imaginative play that comes after the puppets are created.

Straw Bracelets

Materials:

- Straws cut into one inch lengths

- Pipecleaners

Target skills:

- Fine motor skills

- Patterning

- counting

A super simple bin like this is always a huge hit. I love this Quiet Bin for so many reasons.

First of all it is oh so simple to set up and the kids just love it. Even the cutting of the straws is a great hand strengthening activity for little ones.

Second of all, you can use it to strengthen so many different skills.

If your little one is working on counting, challenge them to build bracelets with a certain number of straws. Working on patterns? Add in a few different colours of straws.

Popsicle Stick Houses

Materials:

- Popsicle Sticks

Target skills:

- Imaginative play

- Problem solving

- Patterning and math skills

Pop in a few little people or animals with this bin and you have got everything you need to make houses, barns, schools, you name it.

Simple is best for stretching little ones imaginations and improving creativity. A simple square made out of popsicle sticks can be anything—a house, school, mall, doctors office—anything!

Older children can work on building structures by stacking the popsicle sticks and patterning them to make higher buildings.

Cupcake Liner Butterflies

Materials:

- Clothespins
- Cupcake Liners

Target skills:

- Fine motor skills
- Symmetry
- Colour recognition
- Hand strengthening
- Imaginative play

Little ones will love creating oodles of colourful butterflies with this simple Quiet Bin.

Having one butterfly already made in this bin will help little ones get inspired to create these little creatures.

Not only will those little hands get some great strengthening, those little minds will be differentiating between different colours, and practicing math skills too.

And after they are created? Why that is when all that fabulous imaginative play will take flight.

Button Toss

Materials:

- Buttons

- Cupcake Liners

Target skills:

- Fine motor skills

- Hand-eye coordination

- Counting

Challenge those competitive little souls with this awesome button toss Quiet Bin.

Little ones can set up cupcake liners near and far and try to toss those buttons to land in the liners.

Add some numbers to those cupcake liners for an added challenge for older children.

Depending on your children this might make a great joint Quiet Bin. It would NOT in my house though … there would be nothing quiet about the arguments that would certainly occur.

Clear the Road!

Materials:

- Pompoms
- Clothespins

Target skills:

- Fine motor skills
- Hand Strengthening
- Imaginative play

Oh no! There was a terrible pompom snow-storm and all the snow ploughs are busy!

(Well, they are not busy necessarily, but they are not part of the nine items from the dollarstore—so for the sake of my book, they are busy)

The only way to clear the road is by using clothespins! Luckily, little ones love a job like this and will certainly be up to the task.

Add in some cupcake liners for sorting those pompom snowballs by colour and you have one heck of a Quiet Bin.

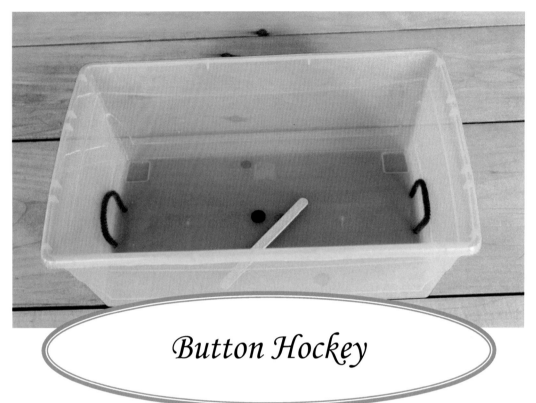

Button Hockey

Materials:

- Pipecleaners
- Button
- Popsicle Stick

Target skills:

- Fine motor skills
- Counting

Now this Quiet Bin will not be for every child, but for my Benjamin it is the ONLY Quiet Bin. Therefore, it simply had to be included.

If you have a hockey fan, then I have the bin for you.

Little ones can use the popsicle stick to score the button puck into the pipecleaner nets.

This is a great chance to sneak in some counting as little ones keep track of their goals.

Pompom Sort

Materials:

- Pompoms of different sizes and colours

- Straw

Target skills:

- Sorting

- Colour recognition

Children learn with their whole bodies. So why not blow through a straw to sort those pompoms?

Little ones will even learn about the power of wind and breath control, as well as learning about differences.

If they are sorting by colour, they will learn that a big red pompom can be in the same group as a little red pompom.

But if sorting by size, those same pompoms would be in different groups.

Big learning from such a little Quiet Bin!

"Art has the role in education of helping children become more like themselves, instead of more like everyone else."

-Sydney Gurewitz Clemens

Letter Formation

Materials:

- Paper plates with letters drawn on

- Buttons

Target skills:

- Letter formation

- Name recognition

This Quiet Bin is best started with a child's name. Beginning alphabet recognition and letter formation with the letters in a child's name is absolutely the way to go.

Popping letters on paper plates using a permanent marker and having little ones trace those lines with buttons is a great way for little ones to practice forming those letters.

They will be strengthening those little fingers too. Once they are comfortable tracing the letters on the plates, they can try to form them independently on the floor using the buttons.

Letter Match

Materials:

- Paper plate
- Clothespins

Target skills:

- Letter matching
- Hand strengthening

Using this Quiet Bin can be done with little ones of any age, really. But to use this bin as I am suggesting (matching uppercase letters to lowercase letters) it is best left to older kids.

Young children can practice matching their name letters—Uppercase on the plate to lowercase on the clothespins.

And of course the possibilities are really endless—you could even practice numbers by writing numerals on the clothespins and dots on the plates.

Adding, subtracting, sight words, you name it!

Paper Plate 3D Art

Materials:

- Paper Plates
- Pipecleaners

Target skills:

- Fine motor skills
- Creativity

My little ones love art—but fitting that into a Quiet Bin, or at least a mess-free Quiet Bin, is a challenge.

This 3D paper plate art is a great compromise.

My little ones can still create unique, child-directed art, while staying independent. No tape, glue, or paint needed.

I simply put oodles of hole punches, or pokes with a sharp pencil, into paper plates which made threading and weaving pipe-cleaners nice and simple.

And they turn out beautiful too!

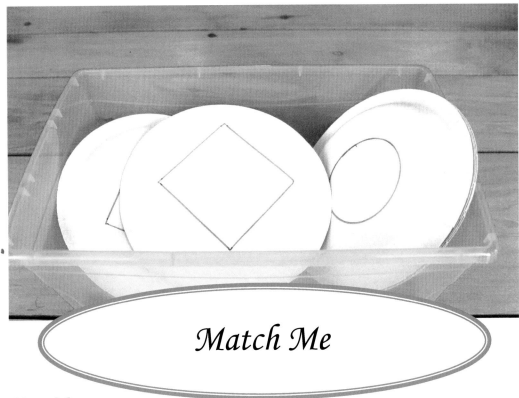

Match Me

Materials:

- Paper plates with shapes drawn on.

Target skills:

- Discerning pictures
- Memory
- Any academic skill!

This Quiet Bin is great for working on so many skills. Simply add matching shapes, numbers, letters, or anything else to the bottom of the paper plates.

Little ones can lay out all the plates, flip over 2 plates at a time and try to find the matches.

Of course children might choose to use this bin in loads of different ways, which is absolutely fine. Creating their own games is another fabulous skill for children to develop.

Button Towers

Materials:

- Buttons

Target skills:

- Ordering
- Patterns
- Coutning

I almost didn't include this Quiet Bin because I thought it was too simple.

But then I realized—when you are talking about busy Mamas—there is no such thing as too simple!

So going on this philosophy that simpler is better, I bring you the simplest of all Quiet Bins: a button box.

Children can stack them into towers, order them by size, make pictures or shapes, and do a million other things as well.

Pompom Soup

Materials:

- Large and small pompoms
- Cupcake liners

Target skills:

- Imaginative play

Now this Quiet Bin really is best if you add in one more supply—but since it is a regular household item I feel okay tossing it in—I hope you feel okay about it too. If not, just wait until your little ones get absorbed in this fabulous imaginative Quiet Bin … I do believe all will be forgiven.

After all, it's just a spoon. Letting little ones scoop up pompoms to serve as soup in little cupcake liner bowls is a hit with all those little aspiring chefs out there.

And when quiet time is over, if you've played your cards right, you might just get offered a cup of pompom soup. Yum!

Cupcake Flowers

Materials:

- Cupcake liners

- Pipecleaners

Target skills:

- Fine motor skills

- Creativity

For this Quiet Bin I like to trim the cupcake liners just a little. Add a few snips and shape a few petals. Older children can do this all on their own.

Though there is no real need, this activity still works with regular cupcake liners.

Simply put a hole punch (or push a pencil tip) through the center of the cupcake liners so little ones can thread them onto green pipecleaners.

Voila! Beautiful flowers

Pipecleaner Jewellery

Materials:

- Cut pipecleaners

Target skills:

- Fine motor skills

- Hand strengthening

- Patterning or counting

My little ones love making pipecleaner chains (which you might recall from my first Quiet Bins book, *A Year of Educational Quiet Bins*).

My 6 year old recently started chopping those pipecleaners into smaller pieces and making tiny pipcleaner chains.

He made those into bracelets and necklaces.

Pretty great idea, right?

See? Quiet Bins grow clever kids.

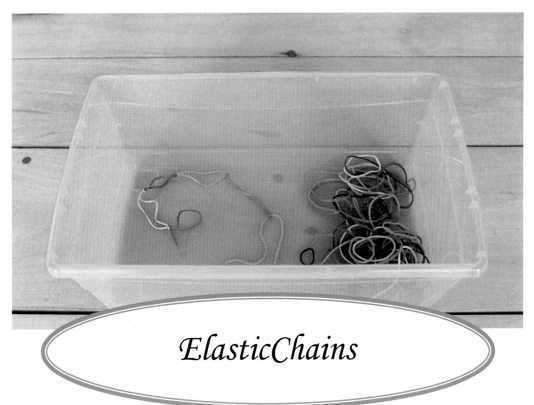

ElasticChains

Materials:

- Elastics

Target skills:

- Fine motor skills

- Patterning and sequencing

Rubberbands can easily be connected by threading a closed band through an open one, opening the closed one and pulling it through itself. It is actually waaaaay easier than that description.

Play with them for a minute and I'm sure you'll see, if this is a new idea to you.

Little ones also pick up on this quick. These rubberband chains can get super long over a quiet time,

We have had some awesome jump ropes created. And one chain as long as the family room!

Pompom Sling Shot

Materials:

- Elastics

- Pompoms

- Clothespins

Target skills:

- Mostly Super FUN

- STEM skills

Well, this one almost certainly will not be quiet. But it's independent and incredibly awesome.

Cut some rubber bands and attach an end to each side of the quiet bin securing with clothespins. Then let those pompoms fly!

While this Quiet Bin (well, um—Bin) is loads of fun, it is also full of learning.

Using different thicknesses and lengths of elastics will help little ones learn about what makes the pompoms go the farthest.

"In this modern world where busyness is
stressed to the point of mania, quietness as
a childhood need is too often overlooked."

-Margaret Wise Brown

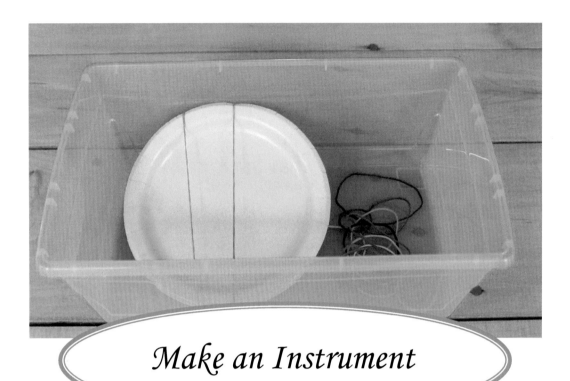

Make an Instrument

Materials:

- Paper plates

- Rubber bands

Target skills:

- Hand strengthening

- Creativity

- Musical awareness

Get ready to get your groove on. Oh goodness my 13 year old will cringe when she reads that!

Stretching elastics over those paper plates will let little ones thrum and strum all day long.

Lots of learning will be happening too as little ones explore different sizes and thicknesses of elastics and paper plates.

Silly Faces

Materials:

- Paper plates
- Pompoms
- Pipecleaners

Target skills:

- Fine motor skills
- Learning about emotions

Draw some great big eyes (or tiny eyes, or winking eyes) onto some paper plates and let the silly face making begin.

Pompom noses, pipecleaner mouths and hair, and you have got some giggling kids.

This Quiet Bin is a great way for little ones to learn about different emotions.

When a face is angry, eyebrows are usually down, mouths will be turned down, and eyes will look narrowed. When happy, those features will look very different.

Counting Cupcake Liners

Materials:

- Cupcake liners
- Buttons
- Pompoms

Target skills:

- Counting
- Fine motor skills

Another crazy simple Quiet Bin that always ends up being one of the most loved.

Pop some cupcake liners in a bin with buttons and pompoms and just watch as all that learning and quiet play unfolds.

You can kick this Quiet Bin up a notch by adding some numbers to the inside of the cupcake liners. This might encourage your little one to practice counting and increase one-to-one correspondence too.

In my house this Quiet Bin always amazes me. Pictures are made, lunch is served, and structures are built, all with this one bin.

Cutting Bin

Materials:

- Cupcake liners
- Scissors

Target skills:

- Scissor skills
- Creativity

Holding and cutting with scissors is an important skill for little ones to master. And like anything, the more they play with the skill, the better.

This Quiet Bin is perfect for those practicing scissor skills. From cupcake liners little ones can practice snipping and chopping easily. The material is sturdy enough to make cutting easy, but thin enough to make more complicated cuts possible too.

Whirligigs, snowflakes, flowers, sunshines, stars—or just some good old fashioned chops.

Ladybug Match

Materials:

- Paper plates

Target skills:

- Counting

This Quiet Bin takes just a minute or two to set up.

Take a paper plate and draw a zigzag or wavy line down the middle. On one half write a number, and on the other half draw the corresponding number of dots. Snip those ladybugs in half and pop them into this bin.

Since each line cut will be different, this is a self-correcting activity.

There will be oodles of counting, one-to-one correspondence, and number recognition with this Quiet Bin.

Tambourine Bin

Materials:

- Paper plates
- Pipecleaners
- Buttons

Target skills:

- Creativity
- Problem solving
- Fine motor skills
- Rhythm and movement

I thought for awhile about how I could make this Quiet Bin completely independent because that is, after all, the entire point of these bins.

The issue I was having was securing the two paper plates together. But I have found a way!

Adding hole punches around the outside of the plates lets little ones thread pipecleaners through easily and twist to secure. After that, it's just popping in a few buttons.

This bin is a great challenge for older children.

Ring Toss

Materials:

- Paper plates
- Clothespins

Target skills:

- Gross motor skills
- Hand-eye coordination

Clip those clothespins onto the sides of the Quiet Bin and let the good times fly!

This Quiet Bin is great for busy little ones. My boys both love it.

I have watched them both add in various challenges for themselves. How far away they can be while still getting it on the clothespin, how many they can get on before the clothespin falls off, and even sorting by colours.

Loads of learning to be had with this one.

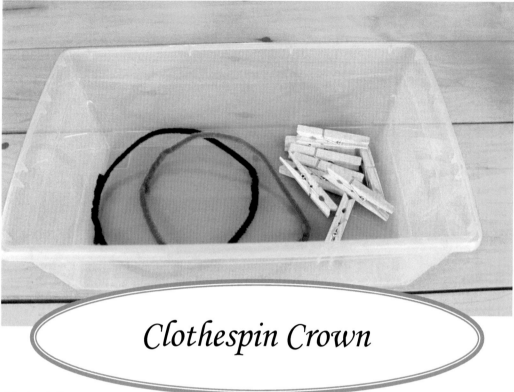

Clothespin Crown

Materials:

- Pipecleaners
- Clothespins

Target skills:

- Imaginative play
- Hand strengthening

This was in fact one of the very first Quiet Bins that ever existed in our house. And like all really good ideas, it came from my two year old.

I wrapped two pipecleaners together so they fit on top of his head like a crown. Next, he grabbed a cup of clothespins and got busy decorating.

And that was all it took for him to become King! Loads of imaginative play happened right after, and the wheels began turning in this Mama's head about the power of Quiet Bins.

Make a Letter

Materials:

- Popsicle sticks

- Pipecleaners

Target skills:

- Letter formation

Did you know that all letters can be formed with a combination of popsicle sticks and pipe-cleaners? They totally can.

Cutting some popsicle sticks in half is a great way to help little ones learn about sizes of lines in the letters too.

I like to add in some alphabet cards or even just the alphabet letters written on piece s of paper with this bin. This will help little ones remember exactly how the letters look.

Of course, a great way to start is by putting your child's name letters in the bin.

Button Wreaths

Materials:

- Pipecleaners

- Buttons

Target skills:

- Fine motor skills

I really like this Quiet Bin as it can be used with little ones of so many different ages.

Tiny little ones can practice just threading a pipecleaner through a hole of a button. Older little ones can thread up one side of the button and down the other so the buttons lay flat. And the oldest of little ones can practice layering the buttons, stacking them, and making very cool 3D wreaths.

These look really pretty hung on a Christmas tree.

Inventors Bin

Materials:

- All 10 Dollarstore Items!

Target skills:

- Creativity and everything else imaginable

I have saved the very best for last. This inventors Quiet Bin is not only the easiest to set up (just pop everything into the Quiet Bin), it is also the most full of learning.

When little ones can create all on their own, without any directions or instructions, really deep learning can occur.

We have a Quiet Bin available like this all the time. And I keep adding to it when I find neat things. An empty roll of tape, a neat little box, small springs, a piece of sponge—anything goes.

"We learn to do something by doing it.
There is no other way."

-John Holt

ABOUT THE AUTHOR

Sarah Noftle is a Mama, Teacher, and Wanna-be Farmer (in that order). Having taught in the kindergarten classroom for many years, she opted to stay home with her own wild ones for awhile. Sarah now balances (sort of) being home with her children and working in the classroom part-time. She has a slight (not slight) chicken obsession, and shares her farm happily with 18 feathery ladies ... oh, and her husband and 3 children.

Sarah currently has two other books, both available on Amazon.com, Amazon.ca, and directly on her blog:

A Year of Educational Quiet Bins: The secret to peaceful days at home with kids

Clever's New Trick: A social story to teach children to stop, think, and make good choices.

Visit her blog at: www.HowWeeLearn.com

Made in the USA
Middletown, DE
21 March 2017